# FRIENDS ARE GOOD

Compiled by Dan Zadra
Designed by Steve Potter

COMPENDIUM®
INCORPORATED

ACKNOWLEDGEMENTS

These quotations were gathered lovingly but unscientifically over several years and/or were contributed by many friends or acquaintances. Some arrived—and survived in our files—on scraps of paper and may therefore be imperfectly worded or attributed. To the authors, contributors and original sources, our thanks, and where appropriate, our apologies. –The Editors

Compiled by: Dan Zadra
Designed by: Steve Potter

ISBN: 978-1-932319-90-3

3rd printing. Printed in China with soy inks.

FRIENDSHIP IS A GREAT PLACE. I'M GLAD WE'RE HERE.

Cat Davis

**Among life's GREATEST GIFTS are THE FRIENDS who know and care about us.**

Gayle Larson

IT'S NOT WHAT WE HAVE
**IN OUR LIFE,**
BUT WHO WE HAVE
**IN OUR LIFE**
**THAT COUNTS.**

J. M. Laurence

**WHILE THE RIGHT FRIENDS ARE NEAR US, WE FEEL THAT ALL IS WELL. OUR EVERYDAY LIFE BLOSSOMS SUDDENLY INTO BRIGHT POSSIBILITIES.**

**Helen Keller**

Anything,
everything,
little or big

**becomes** an adventure **WHEN THE** RIGHT PERSON **SHARES IT.**

Kathleen Norris

# WHAT THE HEART REMEMBERS MOST

**ARE MOMENTS SHARED.**

Elizabeth Browne

We have been

# FRIENDS
# TOGETHER

in sunshine and in shade. Caroline Norton

**We can** ALWAYS DEPEND **on some people to make the best, instead of the worst, of whatever happens.**

Sandra Wilde

# THERE ARE
# PEOPLE
# WHO TAKE THE
# HEART
## OUT OF YOU, AND THERE ARE PEOPLE WHO PUT IT BACK.

Elizabeth David

Whether near or far apart,
**GOOD FRIENDS**
can always find a
way to communicate,
**HEART TO HEART.**

**Dan Zadra**

GOOD FRIENDS are like stars.

You don't always see them,
but you know they are always there.
Unknown

**AMONG THOSE**
WHOM I LIKE OR ADMIRE,
I CAN FIND NO COMMON
DENOMINATOR; BUT AMONG THOSE
**WHOM I LOVE, I CAN:**
**ALL OF THEM**
**MAKE ME LAUGH.**

W.H. Auden

**That is the best—** to laugh with someone because **you both think the same things are funny.**

**Gloria Vanderbilt**

**FRIENDS ARE ALWAYS FRIENDS NO MATTER HOW FAR YOU HAVE TO TRAVEL BACK IN TIME.**

Kellie O'Connor

I can talk to certain people after years and it will seem as if we talked **ONLY YESTERDAY.**

**Tote Yamada**

Everyone hears what you say. Friends actually listen to

what you say. Best friends listen to what you don't say.

Unknown

# A FRIEND IS SOMEONE WHO MAKES IT EASY TO

# BELIEVE IN
# YOURSELF.

Heidi Wills

**Friends are kind to each other's hopes. They cherish each other's DREAMS.**

Henry David Thoreau

**I WISH YOU
ALL THE JOY THAT
YOU CAN WISH.**
William Shakespeare

# ALL I WANT FOR YOU IS THE BEST OF EVERYTHING.

**Veronica Lake**

The best thing to hold
on to in life is each other.
**Audrey Hepburn**

**OUR FRIENDSHIP WILL ENDURE AS LONG AS YOU WISH IT TO.**

Barbara Armand

Hold a true friend

# with both your hands.

African proverb

Favorite people, favorite places
Favorite memories of the past.
These are the joys of a lifetime
These are the things that last.

Unknown

TREASURE
EACH OTHER
IN THE RECOGNITION
THAT WE DO NOT KNOW
HOW LONG WE SHALL
HAVE EACH OTHER.

Joshua Loth Liebman

"I don't think I'll last forever," said Peach. "That's okay," said Blue. "Not many folks do. But until then, YOU HAVE ME, AND I HAVE YOU."

Sarah S. Kilborne

# THANK YOU FOR BEING.

Native American saying